D0946528

Originally published in France under
title *Mukashi, Mukashi*
1863-1883

Copyright © Les Editions Arthaud, Paris, 1984

English translation by Linda Coverdale
© Copyright 1986 by Friendly Press, Inc.
All rights reserved.

First Published in the USA in 1986 by
Friendly Press, Inc.
401 Park Avenue South,
New York City, NY 10016, United States of America
Printed in France
Designed by Marty Goldstein

Library of Congress Cataloging in Publications Data
Beato, Felice, B. CA. 1825.
Once upon a time.
"Passages from Pierre Loti"—T.P. Verso.
Translation of Mukashi, mukashi, 1863-1883.
1. Japan—Description and travel—1801-1900—
Views. I. Stillfried, Raimund, Baron von 1839-1911.
II. Loti, Pierre, 1850-1923. III. Title.
DS809B4313 1986   952   86-7545
ISBN 0-914919-07-5

Passages from Pierre Loti

The photographs reproduced in this book
are the property of the Société de Géographie in Paris,
where the collection is housed in the Bibliothèque Nationale.

Because the photographs came from the same studio
and were not credited to Beato or Stillfried,
credits on the captions were suggested by Chantal Edel.

Once

upon

a

time

Once

upon

a

time

Visions

of

old

Japan.

Photographs

by

Felice

Beato

and

Baron

Raimund

von

Stillfried.

And

the

words

of

Pierre

Loti.

Introduction

by

Chantal

Edel.

Translated

by

Linda

Coverdale.

It was in 1542 that the first European sailing ship, driven off course by a storm, landed on the shores of Japan at Tanegashima. Word of this landfall soon spread throughout Europe, bringing merchants and Christian missionaries in its wake. The former set up shop with no difficulty and soon prospered, while the latter converted hundreds of thousands of Japanese souls. ❊ The accession to power of the Tokugawa Shogunate in 1573 put an end to the spiritual invasion by forcing renunciation or death upon most Christian converts. At the same time, a commercial experiment was ended by a decision to close down the new foreign businesses. Thus, isolated from the outside world by a rigidly authoritarian regime, Japan was to disappear from the economic and political life of the globe for more than two centuries. ❊ During this period the only Western observers of the nation's history and civilization were the Dutch, who were permitted to maintain commercial relations with Japan but who were confined to Deshima, a small island under virtual quarantine in a roadstead near Nagasaki. Through this little window on the world, Western advances in mathematics, geography, medicine, and perhaps the first photographic equipment were introduced into Japan. The first known photographs were taken in 1853 by the daguerreotyper J. Brown, who accompanied American Commodore Matthew Perry on his diplomatic mission to Japan. He took a series of pictures that were, unfortunately, destroyed by fire in London a few years later. ✱ Japan finally emerged from its self-imposed isolation in 1856 when the first consul general of the United States, Townsend Harris, obtained the ratification of a series of treaties permitting the re-establishment of political, commercial, and cultural relations between the two nations. The years that followed were turbulent ones, full of unrest caused by the arrival of foreigners in the newly opened cities and ports, principally Yokohama, Edo, and Nagasaki. ✱

The outbreak of unrest in a remote country could only prove irresistible to an adventurer like Felice Beato, one of the nineteenth century's greatest pioneers of combat photojournalism. Beato was at that time in China, where he had joined the Franco-British expeditionary force in order to cover the last battles of the Opium War. ✳ Judging from the accounts given by his contemporaries, the life of Felice Beato was full of incident. Born in Venice around 1825, he began his career as a photographer in 1850 in Malta. There he met James Robertson, another photographer, who later became his brother-in-law. When Robertson was named chief engraver of the Imperial Mint of Constantinople, Beato accompanied him to his new post. ✳ A chance event led him to take up combat photography when Robert Fenton, who had been sent from England to photograph the Crimean War, became ill and was replaced by James Robertson and Felice Beato in September, 1855. It was probably following the successful London exhibition of the superb photographs they took of the last battles in the Crimea that Felice Beato was made a naturalized English subject. ✳ The two men then crisscrossed the Near East, publishing albums of photographs signed Robertson and Beato. Accompanied by his brother, Antonio Beato, they set out next for India where they followed the movements of the British army around the restless subcontinent. While Antonio and James opened a studio, Felice dramatized on glass plates scenes of horror from the Indian Mutiny, which can be particularly seen in his photographs of Lucknow at the time of the severe British reprisals in 1858. These were the first images of war to show real corpses. ❁ Two years later, Beato did another series of photographs while accompanying the Franco-British expeditionary force in China, where he was present at the attack on Fort Taku and once more worked on the battlefield itself. Here, Beato met the sketch-artist Charles Wirgman, a correspondent for *The Illustrated London News*. Working as they both did on the same subjects, the two men formed ties of mutual respect and deep friendship. ❁ Charles Wirgman left for Japan in the summer of 1861 as a "special artist" for *The Illustrated London News*. From his base in Yokohama, Wirgman sent his newspaper regular reports and illustrations of Japan. There was such a wealth of exciting material that Wirgman urged his friend to come join him, which Beato did in 1863. ❁ Together they founded the first English-language Japanese magazine, *Japan Punch*, which later became *Far East* and continued to appear until 1876. It was quite an accomplishment to have succeeded in making fashionable a style of journalism far removed from the Japanese spirit, especially in a land where foreigners were still a novelty, and a mistrusted one at that. ❁ At the same time, the two men pooled their remarkable talents and set up a photography business in the Yokohama Foreign Settlement, which they managed jointly until 1869. "Signor Beato" introduced this new art form to the Japanese and built up what were in effect documentary archives on the manners and customs of a country in the midst of far reaching changes. Wirgman, a renowned water colorist, hand tinted Beato's finished prints. ✹ Photography was not completely unknown in Yokohama, however. One Shimooka Renjo had been working there with reasonable success since 1859, and in addition, certain amateur photographers had learned this new technique in the course of their official visits to Europe or the United States. Nevertheless, according to a letter from Wirgman published in *The Illustrated London News* of September 26, 1863, the photography studio he had opened with Beato was the immediate object of great public curiosity: "My house is inundated with Japanese officers who come to see my sketches and my companion Signor Beato's photographs. They are extremely polite and bring presents of fruit, paper, and fans. Tomorrow the present regiment leaves, and officers of the new one just arrived have already paid us a visit." ✹ Although photography made rapid strides in Japan, the Japanese were reluctant to accept the principle of the process itself, convinced as they were that the camera possessed the magic power to kill them by absorbing their souls. They called it the "Murder box invented by iniquitous Christians." Aimé Humbert reports this incident in *Le Japon:* "As Beato was preparing to photograph Prince Arima's palace, two of the prince's officers ran up to advise him to stop what he was doing. Monsieur Metman asked them if they would be so kind as to seek specific instructions from their master, which they did, returning within a few minutes. 'The prince absolutely forbids you to take any photograph whatsoever of his palace,' they shouted in one voice. Bowing respectfully, Beato ordered his assistants to dismantle the apparatus, and the officers withdrew satisfied, without suspecting that the photographer had had ample time to take two pictures during their absence." ✹ The fear inspired by this magical machine was compounded by the prohibition against reproducing anything of a sacred character, such as the shogun, the imperial families, or their residences. While accompanying the English Minister Parkes on a diplomatic visit in 1867, Beato did succeed in photographing the shogun, despite having been formally forbidden to do so. The sale of the photographs, however, was prohibited. ✹ As more and more Japanese learned about the art of photography, they quickly began to accept it. In 1871, Baron Hübner wrote: "We are on our way to visit once more the great temple at Asakusa, one of the marvels of Edo. Climbing a few steps, we find ourselves in a long, narrow street lined with shops and teahouses that leads straight to the grand entrance of the temple. Here may be purchased votive paintings on blessed paper, holy images, all sorts of profane articles, photographic views and portraits. The Japanese are past masters in this art, which has taken root here within the space of a few years and is practiced today in localities as yet unseen by any European…"

✳ The studio opened by Beato and Wirgman flourished handsomely, especially as they had adopted the European procedure of hand painting on prints. Indeed, in 1862 the Japanese had reacted to black-and-white photography in the same way as had Europeans confronted with the first photograph: with regret that the reproduction of forms and features could not also show color. ✳ As early as 1816 the inventor of photography, Niepce, had been seeking to obtain an image "that would paint itself on the paper in its natural colors." The nineteenth century saw many subsequent experiments along these lines, from Daguerre to Ducos du Hauron. The disappointing results of these experiments, however, resulted in the temptation to paint directly on photographs, a technique that was largely the domain of the fashionable artists of the day. ✳ In order to gratify a public accustomed to the attractions of the miniature, a number of daguerreotypers colored portraits taken on silvered photographic plates. There were various methods of applying this hand coloring, often performed by talented painters. The tinted photographs were carefully framed and often placed in small slip cases or caskets for better protection. This *coloriage* quickly became quite popular. ❋ Although Beato made no contribution to true color photography, it was his idea to have Wirgman tint his photographs with the same dyes and paints used by Japanese artists. The two were quickly overwhelmed by the demand for their work and so began hiring local painters who were particularly skillful at achieving the subtle coloring of Japanese prints. A photograph taken by Beato entitled "My Artist" shows his usual painter, pince-nez on the bridge of his nose, brush in one hand, the black-and-white print to be colored in the other. ❋ Beato and Wirgman lived in Japan during particularly troubled and xenophobic times. Indeed, they each had a close brush with death during this period. On the night of July 5, 1861, Wirgman barely escaped from a band of reactionary samurai besieging the British embassy. As for Beato, Francis Adams relates in his *History of Japan* that a few years later the photographer very nearly accompanied Major Baldwin, whom he had met in Enoshina, on an excursion to Kamakura, but in the end he decided not to go along. When he heard that Baldwin had been assassinated in Kamakura by samurai opposed to the presence of foreigners in Japan, Beato could hardly believe it and took his revenge by photographing the execution of the murderer, Shimidzu Seiji. ✳ In contrast to his earlier experiences as a photojournalist, Felice Beato had little occasion while he was in Japan to photograph scenes of a sensational nature, aside from crucifixions (the traditional punishment for regicides) or the decapitations of prisoners condemned for murder. He was not in Shimonoseki during the bloody events of 1864 and was only able to record a vast panoramic view of the scene after the battle. ✳ On the other hand, he discovered within himself a commensurate talent for photographing typical Japanese scenes. This same taste for authenticity, which had led him to preserve forever the image of soldiers killed but a few hours before on the battlefield, was now devoted to the composition of scenes from Japanese life. His body of work is like one vast panorama of the country. ✳ Beato's first series of photographs was published in 1868 in two albums entitled *Photographic Views of Japan with Historical and Descriptive Notes, Compiled from Authentic Sources, and Personal Observations During a Residence of Several Years.* The first volume, *Views of Japan,* essentially comprises shots of landscapes, villages, and cities taken during trips made in the company of other travelers or in the retinue of a visiting dignitary. The second volume, *Native Types,* is a much more representative collection of his personal work. In it, Beato offers us his "historical" vision of a country changing before his very eyes, inspiring him to attempt to capture with each shot everything that would soon vanish, those objects and traditions doomed to fall by the wayside. These images of geishas, samurai, wrestlers, and small craftsmen are not so much portraits as they are an essay on the classes of Japaneses society. Each shot is like a canvas painted by Japanese artists—those uncontested masters of the print—so that Beato's photographs might be the most faithful possible reflection of his vision of Japan. ❧ The great fire that ravaged Yokohama in 1866 destroyed some of Beato's photographs, despite the fact, as Charles Wirgman reported in *The Illustrated London News*, that they had been careful to keep them in supposedly fireproof tin trunks. The fires that spread so quickly through the many little wooden houses of the city posed a constant danger in Yokohama. This loss was all the more regrettable in that these documents were records of ancestral traditions still observed under the last shoguns. Fortunately, the two men were quickly able to rebuild their collection of photographs, since there was no lack of new subjects and opportunities. It must be remembered that the purpose of their firm was the commercialization in the West of that great novelty, *japonisme*, the craze for all things Japanese. Their work was widely circulated within Japan as well as abroad in the form of illustrations for contemporary books and magazines on Japan, or in albums that were truly travelogues. ❧ When

Baron von Stillfried bought out the firm of Beato and Wirgman in 1877, the two former associates were no longer working together. By that time, Wirgman was plying his talents as a journalist and sketch artist. As for Felice Beato, for a while he turned his hand to dealing in objets d'art before returning one last time to war photography in the Sudan (1885-1886), which he covered in the company of General Wolseley. He ended his days in Burma as an antique dealer, devoting little time to photography. 🍁

21

Baron Raimund von Stillfried und Ratenitz continued the traditions of Beato and Wirgman through the production of genre and documentary photographs, but he added his own personal touch to the firm's repertoire. Because he was first and foremost a painter, imbued with the artistic and cultural heritage of Europe, he composed his pictures with a painter's eye. The eternal feminine was a favorite subject of his, clothing in modesty and serenity even the nude. The very poses of his models evoke the great artistic traditions of his day. 🍁 The little information we have concerning this talented adventurer is derived mostly from biographical accounts dating from the beginning of this century. Born in Bohemia in 1839, this former officer and experienced traveler arrived in Japan for the second time in 1870, after having served in Mexico as a volunteer in the army of the Austrian Emperor Maximilian. For a while he held the post of head of chancery for Northern Germany at the embassy in Tokyo while working also as a businessman and as a reporter for Austria. 🍁 The circumstances leading to his departure from Austria are not known, but perhaps he took part in the "Imperial Austrian Expedition" to Eastern Asia, as did the great photographer Wilhelm Burger, who arrived in Japan in September, 1869. The purpose of the expedition was to bring back objects, documents, information, and photographs from the little-known countries of Asia to provide material for an exhibit at the Museum für Angewandte Kunst (Museum of Applied Arts) in Vienna. ✳ Stillfried probably decided to leave the expedition and stay on for a while in Japan. In 1872 he set up a studio where the future great names in Japanese photography came to be initiated in this new art. Stillfried did not abandon his painting, however, and his prints (which he colored himself) show a Japan already more Westernized than in Beato's time. These photographs were much admired at the Japan Exhibition in Vienna in 1873, enhancing a reputation that would later lead to Stillfried's appointment as photographer to the Austrian court. ✳ Stillfried's studio was reputedly the best in Eastern Asia, although it must be said that at his arrival two years earlier, studio photography was entirely within the hands of a few Europeans. As there was little local competition, the situation could hardly have been more promising. By the time he took over Beato's studio in 1877, Stillfried's reputation was so great that he received a commission from Emperor Mutsu-Hito for a panorama representing Fujiyama for the imperial palace in Tokyo. ✳ Stillfried remained in Japan as an instructor at the State Press until 1883, when he bequeathed the property of the firms of Beato and Wirgman, Stillfried and Andersen to Kusakabe Kimbei, surely the most gifted of his disciples. He made made several trips to Siberia and Hong Kong and then returned to

Vienna where in addition to continuing his work as a painter and photographer, he set up an atelier for the restoration of paintings based on procedures of his own invention. Thus, he acquired new fame abroad and at home in Vienna, where he died in 1911. ✳ With Stillfried, the ascendancy of Europeans in Japanese photography came to an end. Almost everywhere in Japan the Japanese themselves were ready to carry on the photographic work begun by foreigners. ✳

In July 8, 1885, a dashing lieutenant disembarked from La Triomphante in Nagasaki. His name was Julien Viaud, but he was better known by his literary pseudonym, Pierre Loti. He had just made headlines with his dispatches as a correspondent to the Parisian newspaper *Le Figaro* in which he denounced the actions of the French in Hué in 1883. ❧ Steamship navigation and the coming of the railroad had already greatly changed Japan by the time of Loti's arrival. However, like Beato and Stillfried before him, whose albums he must have seen, Loti was interested above all in traditional Japan, a Japan still largely shrouded in mystery. Works written about Japan were excursions into uncharted territory, and Pierre Loti was the first writer whose novels helped launch the grand period of *japonisme*. ❧ Loti's first impressions of Japan were recorded in his novel *Madame Chrysanthème* (1887), a fictionalized transcription of his *Journal de Nagasaki,* his faithfully kept daily diary. The book was a worldwide success and certainly helped to shape an image of Japan that in many ways is still alive today. "In the late 19th century, Loti's Japan became Europe's Japan," said Endymion Wilkinson. Even Van Gogh wrote to his brother Theo: *"Have you read* Madame Chrysanthème? *The fact that true Japanese have nothing on their walls has really made me think—like those descriptions of a cloister or a pagoda where there's nothing to see (the drawings and curios are hidden in drawers!. Ah! That's the way to look at a work of Japanese art, in a well-lighted room, completely bare, open to the landscape."* ✳ A few months later during a trip to Kyoto and Tokyo, Loti wrote *Japoneries d'Automne*, a book inspired by his unabashed worship of the empress of Japan: "Her name is Harou-Ko, which means Springtime." In the book, Loti weighs the importance of having caught a glimpse of her at a time when she was still considered a sacred personage, at the annual Chrysanthemum Festival, where the empress might be briefly approached before an audience of around forty privileged persons. "I admit that I plotted and intrigued to obtain my invitation from this almost invisible empress, whose very invisibility makes me dream of seeing her." ✳ Even though he did not always comprehend the Japanese spirit, Loti felt overwhelmed by some power emanating from the very person of the empress and from all the ceremonies surrounding her fleeting appearance. She was the symbol of the country he was seeking to understand, but a symbol unveiled only briefly, in the shade of an umbrella emblazoned with the imperial arms, in the impressive formality of the traditional gardens: *"The large violet parasol, delightfully embroidered with chrysanthemums, tilted upward and I caught sight of her... Her little painted face chilled and enchanted me. As she passes by, close enough to brush against me, across my chest falls* her shadow, which I would have liked to keep as a rare treasure. I studied her carefully, and she is one of those few women who may be called, in the most refined sense of the word, exquisite. Exquisite and strange, with her air of a cold goddess looking deep within herself, or into the distance, or heaven knows where; exquisite, her eyes, almost closed, seeming in their length like two oblique black lines quite distant from those other two, more slender, lines of her eyebrows…She is a small woman; she walks with a cadenced step, within the scrupulous stiffness of garments that reveal nothing of her delicate figure…At times, when something that has escaped me astonishes or vexes her, the expression on her face changes suddenly; the smile remains, but for an imperceptible instant, a nervous contraction pinches her small aquiline nose, her eyes become ironical, or hard, or cruel; they flash a brief command, a cold flame. And she is more charming then, and more womanly." ✺ Loti's meeting with Harou-Ko inspired his most beautiful pages on Japan, and also his most nostalgic ones, because he already sensed the inevitable change in the air: "And it's also a part of the real Japan that has just vanished there, at that bend in the road, into the eternal night of days gone by—since neither those costumes nor that ceremony will ever be seen again…For the first time in my life, I feel a kind of vague regret thinking about the approaching total eclipse of a civilization that for centuries had been so refined." ✺ Pierre Loti is well aware of discovering a country already influenced by Western modernism (the princes and guests at the festival are in European clothing), but still preserving its native moral and spiritual values (the empress wears traditional Japanese dress). At the same ceremony the following year, little would remain of the ancient rituals. The Chrysanthemum Festival would become a garden party presided over by the empress, resplendent in the latest Parisian fashion. ❦ In another work, *L'Exilée*, a series of essays based on his various journeys in the Orient, Loti continues the theme of loss. Again, he uses the empress as the symbol of old Japan, but this time the words have a melancholy tone, a sense of finality: *"Despite the graciousness of her welcome, one sensed that she was offended by our presence, which had been forced upon her by new customs and conventions, upon her, the sacred empress, a being once invisible, like a religious myth. All that is over and done with now: gone forever the stunning robes of ancient splendor, the great fans of dreamlike beauty, vanished into closets and museums. With one fell blow, the great leveling of modern times has suddenly transformed this Court of the Mikado that had remained until now more inaccessible than a cloister, preserving ancestral rites, costumes, and graces unchanged since time immemorial."* ❦ In his last novels, in particular *L'Exilée* and *La troisième jeunesse de Madame Prune*, Loti has given himself entirely to the past. Present-day

Japan is of little interest to him: "As a child, I had read the story of Chushin-gura, the tale of the forty-seven faithful samurai." Thrilled by the chivalry of these heroes who sacrificed their lives in a cruel hara-kiri to avenge the death of a beloved prince, Loti promised himself that if he ever went to Japan one day, he would go "to pay homage at their tomb…This place truly has a great melancholy all its own. And then the story is so beautiful, to one who knows it well; a story of such astonishing heroism, exaggerated honor, and superhuman fidelity." ✽ He wrote in his private diary on Monday, the first of April, 1901: *"We're leaving this country in its full glory of flowers and springtime…Life was so simple and sweet, in a marvelous setting! And all our little world of friends, gentle, smiling, amusing, had become so familiar to us…"* This entry marked his final visit to Japan. He never re-turned. ✽ In his *Promenades japonaises*, Emile Guimet writes: "When I want to know what France is like, I will read the travel writings of a Japanese. And it's for that very same reason that when a European wants to get to know Japan or any other country in the Orient, he seeks out photographs, travelers' sketches, and the impressions of tourists, confident that these notes taken from day to day will bring the reader himself along on a voyage, giving him his share of pleasures and problems, miscalculations, excitements and disappointments that make up the attraction of a trip around the world." ✳ The photographs of Beato and Stillfried, as well as the writings of Loti, provide more than just travel impressions. It's difficult to imagine the effect the work of these artists had on their generation, but it undoubtedly contributed greatly to the Western infatuation with Japanese art and culture. Their work also shows us that far from being untrue to itself in contact with other civilizations, Japan has remained faithful to the essence of its traditions. ✳ *"It amused me to note down, not unkindly, all these details, which by the way I guarantee are true, like those of a photograph before retouching. In this country that is changing so prodigiously fast, it will perhaps also amuse the Japanese themselves, in a few years, to rediscover this stage in their evolution, written down in these pages."* ✳

PIERRE

LE

COR,

MADAME

CHRYSANTHÈME,

AND

PIERRE

LOTI.

These women have a feeling for the poetry of things, for the vast soul of nature, for the charm cast by flowers, forests, silence, moonbeams…

✳ *They say these things in somewhat mannered verses, as graceful as those leaves or reeds painted on silks and lacquer ware, so natural and yet so fantastic… Might they be like their grandmothers, heroines of poems and courtly legends who valued a point of honor so highly, and revered the ideal of love?* ✳

PORTRAIT

WITH

FAN.

Baron von Stillfried.

TWO

SUMO

WRESTLERS.

Baron von Stillfried.

SUMO

WRESTLERS.

Baron von Sti

835

And finally, in the distance, a bare outline almost lost against that blue of a more and more sovereign hue, appear... these small islands, seeming almost too confident amid the vast surrounding waters, and too pretty, with the cedars on their shores leaning out over the sea... Approaching these summits, one is up above the temples, in a quintessential Japan full of wonders, supremely elegant, serene, almost religious, and one forgets to smile, lost in admiration.

NABAE-SIMA.

Felice Beato (?).

214. NABAE-SIMA

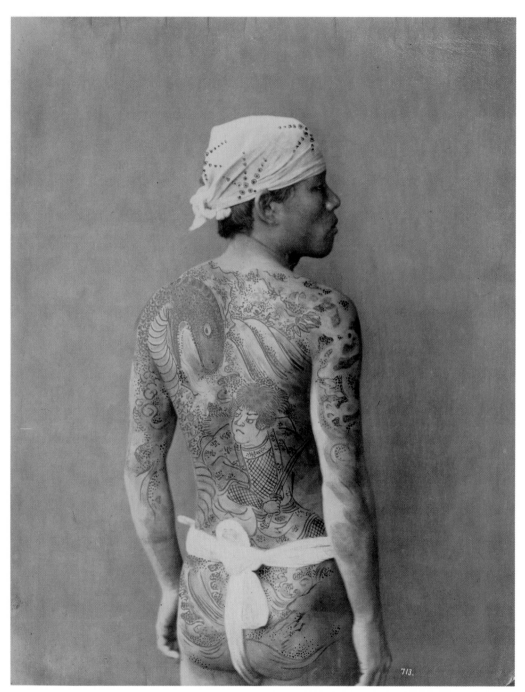

BETTO

(STABLEBOY)

Baron von Stillfried
(after an original
probably
by Felice Beato)

PEDDLER.

Felice Beato.

HEN.

n von Stillfried (?).

YOUNG

WOMAN.

Baron von Stillfried (?).

NIKKO

BRIDGE.

Felice Beato.

Pausing, I admire the curve of this sumptuous bridge, standing out with astonishing elegance against the distant wilderness of the surrounding countryside. The torrent rumbles underneath in a sinister chasm, pouring out white vapor against a bluish backdrop of forests and mountains without a trace of human presence.

Then, remembering certain old pictures preserved in the temples, I try to envision once more, in the midst of this unchanging setting, the processions of long ago crossing over this arc of red lacquer: the war masks, the princes in their terrifying, bizarre magnificence; the emperors whom it was death to gaze upon, surrounded by "warriors with two swords" beheading the curious who dared to look; all that incredible pomp of old Japan, now gone forever beyond the reach of our imagination.

754.

NING

E.

von Stillfried.

SHINTO

PRIEST.

Baron von Stillfried.

747.

47

AT

THE

BARBER'S.

Felice Beato.

557

*F*erreting out trinkets is, I believe, the greatest diversion in this land of Japan. One takes a seat on a mat in the little antique shops to have a cup of tea with the merchants; then one rummages through the cupboards, in the chests, where the old things lie piled up in their absurd extravagance… ✳

AY

MEN

HIWARA

T

RICT).

e Beato.

WOMAN

WITH

MIRRORS.

Baron von Stillfried (?).

OLD

MAN.

Baron von Stillfried.

TOSHO-GU

GATE

AT

NIKKO.

Felice Beato.

*W*ithin, everything is new, airy, polished, elegant: the woodwork is white and fragile, perfectly crafted. ✳ Of course, the walls of the room are only paper partitions. On two sides, opaque paper forms large, solid panels. On the other two partitions, the paper is thin, supported by a grid of light wood that divides it into an infinity of small transparent squares. ✳ That is where light may enter; these delicate frames are also movable, and can be opened like our glazed windows, leading out to verandas that are closed in at night by panels of solid wood, following the universal custom of Japanese houses. ✳ In the foreground is the small garden of the house, with its rockery, its dwarf shrubbery, its ornamental pools, its miniature pagodas. ✳

ODJI.

Felice Beato.

648.

WOMEN

WITH

LACQUERED

TEETH.

Baron von Stillfried (?).

806.

63

YOUNG

WOMAN

FROM

NIIGATA.

Baron von Stillfried (?).

CARPEN

Felice Bee

758.

A tiny little village; the street is wide, but it is the only one, a continuation of the same road I've been following for ten leagues since leaving Utsunomya. Gone are the cedars that loomed over our heads, however, now were under the open sky, breathing an atmosphere much fresher than in Edo, and colder, too: the clean, crisp air of the hills.

🍁 Almost all the little houses belong to merchants selling gray bear skins (the mountains are full of these beasts) and the pelts of a kind of yellow polecat. 🍁 There are also inns, for the pilgrims who are numerous, it seems, in the spring, and shops selling religious articles, tiny gods carved from the white wood of trees from the sacred forest. 🍁 The street slopes gently upward, and towering behind the typically low-roofed houses on each side are the lofty green mountains, crowding close together in the clear sky. 🍁

YUMOTO,

NEAR

NIKKO.

Felice Beato.

YUMOTO. 381.

O

RS.

von Stillfried.

GEISHA.

Baron von Stillfried.

785.

OLD

WOMAN

PEDDLING

FANS

AND

BROOMS.

Felice Beato.

KOREAN

TRAVELE

ON

THE

BRIDGE

OF

A

SHIP.

Felice Be

MONGERS.

e Beato.

RONIN

(MASTERLESS

SAMURAI).

Felice Beato.

*C*rowds of people on this "road to the Eastern Sea," constantly coming and going; merchants' cries, laughter, bustling zeal, heedless fellows running at full speed, bumping into each other, stopping for a minute in front of the inn to bolt down a bowl of rice, a cup of tea—then dashing back again the way they came, as fleet as hares. ✳ A few horses, their harnesses decorated with multicolor ribbons and pendants. But most of all, porters carrying burdens, messengers running, men working at all the tasks of strength and speed that we Europeans consign to beasts… ✳ And the ceaseless stream of common people, carrying packages of rice, bundles of cloth, crates of china on their bamboo poles; enormous porcelain vases for export borne along in procession on human backs, each one swaddled in a straw casing like our bottles of champagne. ✳

TOKAIDO.

374

THE

TOKAIDO

ROAD.

Felice Beato.

PORTER

IN

TRAVELING

CLOTHES.

Felice Beato.

ODD

JOB

MEN.

Felice Be

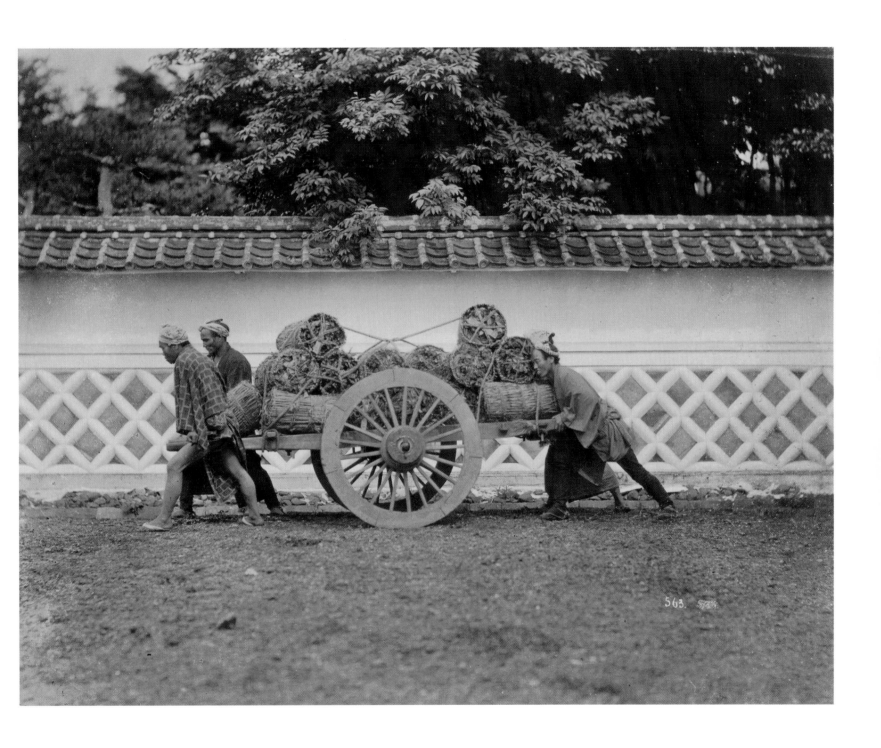

PORTRAIT

OF

A

WOMAN.

Baron von Stillfried.

TEA

VENDOR.

Felice Beato.

HIGH

RANKIN

OFFICER

HORSE.

Felice Be

*O*n the twelfth of November, in this forest that

was once a city, the cicadas are singing everywhere

in the last sunshine of autumn; gerfalcons pierce the

air with their "Haw! Haw! Haw!," that sound so

characteristic of the Japanese countryside, while the

rooks caw mournfully. 🍁 The air is still warm

and the sky unclouded, but the morning chill has already

touched the lotus, which droop their yellowed leaves

above the water. 🍁 A November melancholy deepens

the sadness of dead antiquity one senses all around,

fallen beneath the grass and the moss. 🍁

TOKYO,

"SPECTACLES"

BRIDGE.

Felice Beato.

MEGANE-BASHI 330.

PERSON

IN

WESTERN

DRESS.

Baron von Stillfried.

RESTAURANT.

Baron von Stillfried.

MESSENGER.

Felice Beato.

90

YAKUNIN

(OFFICER).

Baron von Stillfried.

*A*nd then transparent paper panels glide along their grooves, opening to reveal the gardens outside, bathed in peaceful sunshine. The enchantment begins…  Standing on the threshold of this parlor now open to the air, we are on a slight elevation…and through a cluster of low-hanging cedar branches, we glimpse sunken gardens, velvety lawns, strangely shaped rocks, streams flowing under delicate bridges curved in a half-circle, the shimmering of placid water under greenery, paths vanishing deeply into the woods. Scattered on the grass-covered slopes are clumps of "silver bamboo," a verdure almost white in color, "red maples," looking like trees of coral, and some bushes I don't recognize, with leaves the color of purple scabious… There is a particular stillness in these usually impenetrable gardens, a silence all their own, a profound melancholy today made more poignant by the onset of autumn.

GARDEN.

Baron von Stillfried.

602

NNER.

on von Stillfried.

YOUNG

NOBLE

FROM

SAZUMA.

Baron von Stillfried.

THEATRICAL

SCENE.

Baron von Stillfried.

TWO

PORTER

FROM

KAGO.

Felice B

R

OSSING.

e Beato.

THE

ART

OF

KENDO

(A

MAN

AND

A

WOMAN).

Baron von Stillfried.

And it was in the fields and valleys of this pleasant green land that those unparalleled scenes took place—the clash of rival armies, hand-to-hand, outfitted with that demoniac art of theirs, as the long, keen swords whirled about their heads in the two handed grip of short, muscular arms, hacking bloody gashes everywhere, mowing down pell-mell the masked figures and their great horned helmets.

IN
FRONT
OF
HACHIMAN-GU
(THE
TEMPLE
OF
WAR)
IN
TOKYO.
Felice Beato.

STREET

ENTERTAINERS.

Baron von Stillfried (?).

THRESHIN

RICE.

Felice Bea

ARCHER.

Baron
von Stillfried (?).

GOTEN

FUJI-

YAMA.

Felice B

783

GOTEN.

FAMILY

PORTRAIT.

Baron von Stillfried.

TEMPLES

AT

KYOTO.

Felice Beato.

Sheltered by a dense forest on the slopes of the Sacred Mountain of Nikko, surrounded by waterfalls murmuring ceaselessly in the shade of cedars, there is a series of enchanted temples, of bronze and lacquer, with roofs of gold, seemingly conjured up by a magic wand amid ferns and mosses, in the green humidity beneath the vault of darkling boughs, in the middle of the wilderness… ✻ They were strange mystics and rare artists, the men who built such magnificence three or four hundred years ago, in the heart of the forest, to honor their dead. ✻

YOUNG

WOMAN.

Baron von Stillfried.

PRINCE

IN

COURT

DRESS.

Baron von Stillfried.

YOUNG

MOTHER

OUT

FOR

A

WALK.

Felice Beato.